AF432200

TRACK ROAD

Through

A PINE FOREST

A Collection Of Scrapes, Bumps And

Bruises

This Collective is
Dedicated
to **all** the persons that have been bruised,
scratched, scarred and perhaps healed by the
journey through their respective
Pine Forests.
May you never give up.

To Sherry, Beauty And Ruth.

My amazing SAC '96 family that read my
stories and continuously encouraged me.

My dear friend Cecil A. Newry, without you,
these would've remained undiscovered.

CONTENTS:

Introduction

Rambling vivaciously through the

unbridled bushes of life,

one obtains both lessons and rewards.

Here is an eclectic compendium of

beleaguered meditations and

impetuous emotions.

"I stand in safety

Finally so close to civilization

And I look at the jagged jigsaw that I am

And realize a huge part of me is missing

Why?

Because there remains that piece of me

That refused to leave that world,

Those memories

And those feelings…

There's a piece of me

That wanders the woods

Hauntingly

Still looking

For you."

-Incomplete-

LOST

In the dark, I can hear you
But where are you?
You growl my name into the wind
And whisper your desires
Among the leaves
But where are you?

Your scent is intoxicating,
Even in the rain soaked forest,
Filled with flora
And the musk of ferns –
Your scent fills my lungs
I can smell you, but
Where are you?

In the black thick darkness,
I know your eyes are sparkling
I wish I could see them
I'm screaming in silence
Because I know you can hear me.

You were holding - we were
Holding hands
I don't know when it was exactly
That you let go
When it was that the cold
Began to envelop m e

In the midst of my fears
And the unknown
Dangers
That encapsulated me,
You were there,
And now, now that I've
Walked
The last mile through
This dark,
Intolerant forest
To freedom—
Where are you?

I did what I never
Thought I could
All alone on my own,
I still wonder though
Where Are You?

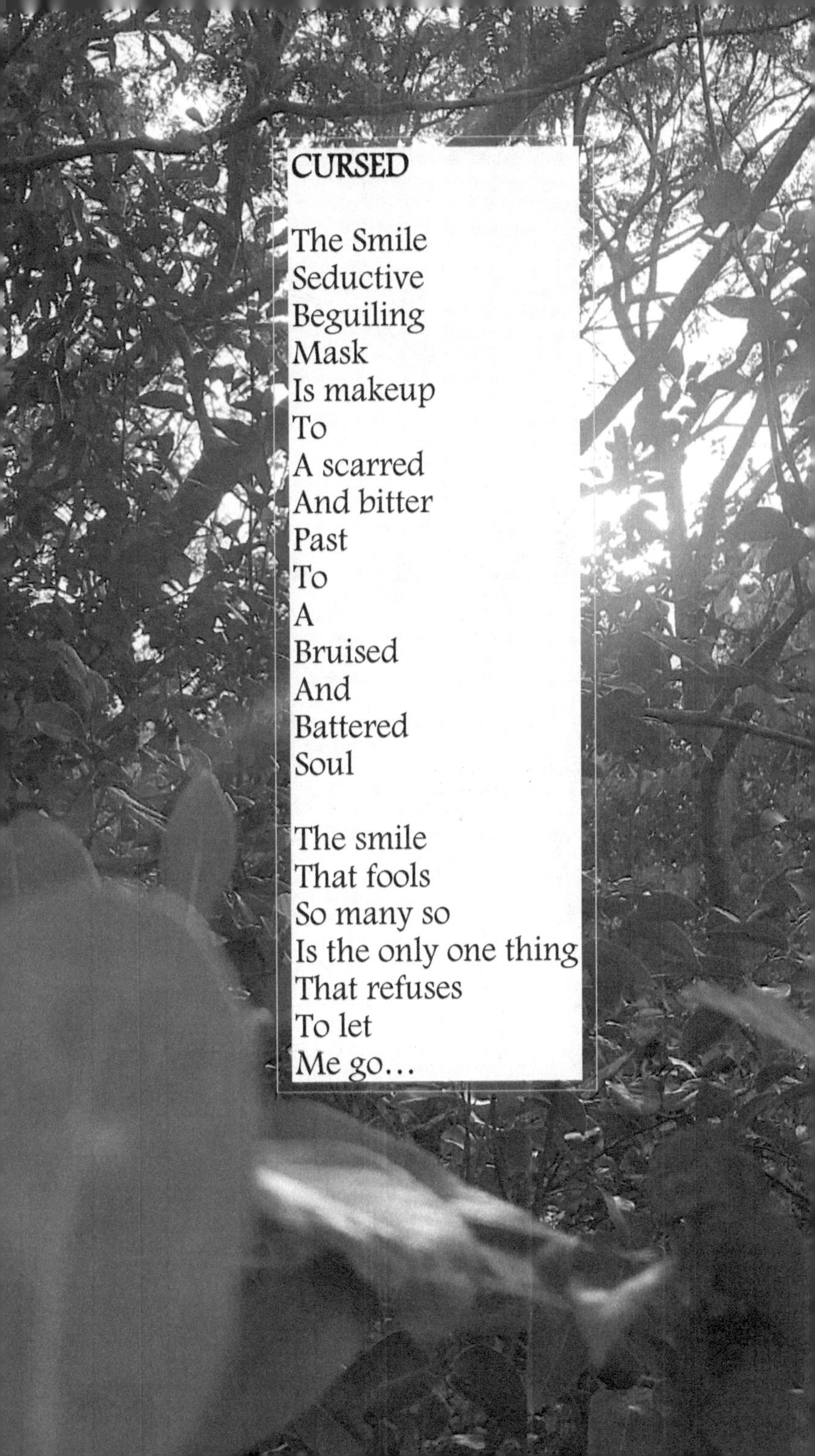

CURSED

The Smile
Seductive
Beguiling
Mask
Is makeup
To
A scarred
And bitter
Past
To
A
Bruised
And
Battered
Soul

The smile
That fools
So many so
Is the only one thing
That refuses
To let
Me go…

WHISPERING DECEIT

Danger is as danger does,
Under the guise of night
When deceit and lies are intertwined
The air is stanched with fright

Forbidden love the sweetest fruit
Oft muddles the mind with lust
A piece of soul
You take with you
With each impassioned thrust

Bodies in darkness
Braving the risks
No care of the choices made
Perilous encounters,
Whispering Deceit
Most trusting of hearts betrayed

Danger is as danger does,
The possibility of harm or death
Beguiling smiles
In danger's eyes
Guaranteed to steal your breath

DISILLUSIONED

You were more than my friend,
        Instead you were my very best
Representation of my true self.
        I entrusted you with the things
Unknown and unseen to many.

I valued your word, your thoughts
And your opinions
And I believed more than the sun rising in
The east
That those courtesies were fully reciprocated

I watched in awe as you broke skin and bled
To mend fractured friendships and
Relationships with those along your
Path;
I admired this trait
Knowing that I, too was worthy of the above
And beyond
I watched in faschination
As you exhausted every adhesive to mend
Often frivolous, faux baubles and Braclelets.

Alas, fate would breathe heavily in your face
With such ferocity

That our necklace fell from your neck
In slow motion, it slid tragically from your
Clavicle in a free fall
Of course, the inevitable would never be

I thought you would catch – us
I waited for you to use outstreched hands to
Save us
You never did.

We fell onto the unforgiving concrete
Our pieces shattering
I thought you would pick us up
Try to salvage all the beautiful jewels that
Made us so precious

Instead, you walked around on the shattered
Beads pretending they weren't crushing and
Crunching under your nonchalantness

The hurt was excruciating
The betrayal numbing
You didn't rush to fix or repair us
And you haphazardly obliterated whatever
Was left

Then one day you were walking past
A few glints of beads caught your eye
You looked down and gathered a few sun~
Bleached pieces
You used an old expired adhesive
You rushed it carelessly
After all you had a life to get back to

Needless to say, our clasp had been broken
And stepped on
It never held the weight
We easily became unglued
What we once had was no more

Now, I can only reminisce
On the days we supported each other
Complimented each other
The days we seemed incomplete without
Each other

Or maybe
Just maybe
Those days only existed only
In my mind's eye

INVASION

I

Was
Playing in the woods
Thick and dark
And deep
As I've done for years
My own playground
My world
Secluded
Desolate

Falling on rocks
Scratched by thorns
Falling out of trees
I'd limp home daily
With fresh wounds
Bleeding hands
And scarred flesh

This was my daily
Yearly norm
When one day
I saw you
Standing there
First~Aid in hand
How you found me
In *my* woods
I did not know

HALLUCINATIONS

Dreams are random
Fragments
Of scenes
We deja vous

Reality swirls in ice cream
Flavors
Of sugared words and hues
And with any luck
The best of dreams
Only if you're one of
The lucky ones
Just could come true

But,
Though we dance on clouds of glitter
Flying into bliss on a
Unicorn's kiss
The reality is
Life's journey has
Taken it's toll on tired feet
Our world is void of sparkle
Bruised and scarred
We slumber oft on a boarded floor

And though
Our heart will always
Chime for the sweet freedom
True love can bring,
Heartbreak
Brings the kind of pain
The body fights to endure
As
Our innocence dies forevermore.

CHOKED

What should I say,
When I can say no more?

What should I say,
When all that I thought we had
Lies shattered on the floor?

What should I say,
When all my screams fall on deaf ears?

What should I say,
When the voice I have left is filled with
tears?

What should I say,
When my throat has uttered all it could?

What would I say,
Truly say
If I could?

ENLIGHTENED ~
Your kisses
Soft and sweet,
Your lips
Give life to
My dying,
Gasping
Soul

Your hands
Warm and gentle
Touches beyond
Skin and flesh
But caresses the very
Fibre of my being
So fresh, so new
   It recharges
   A thirsty heart
      Revives
      A dull ashen flower
         Regenerates
         A hungry spirit
Frees
A caged beast
Transforming a tortured caterpillar
To that of a liberated
Butterfly
Floating
Fluttering
High above the pain
Looking back only once
To blow you a kiss – Goodbye

SMOTHERED

Hand over my nose
I can't breathe

Iron fist clenched over my life
I can't leave

Constant tags on my movements
Is killing me

Ringing my phone til it bleeds
I can't deal

Sometimes,
I want to disappear
Just vanish into thin air
Star-Trekked,
To another time and place
Where I don't exist
And no one knows my name or face

RAGE

I give, give, and give
And yet still
It doesn't seem like
Enough

I

Constantly
Continuously
Consistently
Put others
Before
Self

Only to be
Put
Last
Or
Better yet
Never
At all

So the rage
It bottles up
Because no one
No one

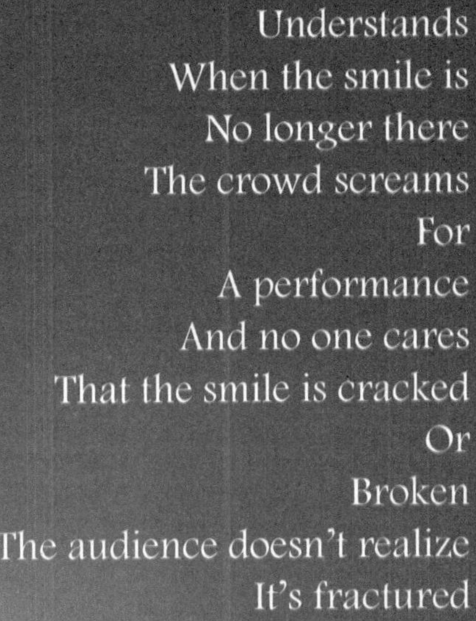

Understands
When the smile is
No longer there
The crowd screams
For
A performance
And no one cares
That the smile is cracked
Or
Broken
The audience doesn't realize
It's fractured

That
Today,
I need
A
Smile

Because
Even when
I have
Nothing
Left to give
They still
Want
More

DISGUST

I miss you
The smell of
Your skin
The taste
Of your
Lips

I miss you
The sound of
Your voice
The
Vibration of
Your laughter

I miss you
The strength of
You – man –
The euphoric
Presence
Your aura had

I miss you
Your inability to
Answer me
Completely
And the half love
You half gave
To
Whole me

DISGUST

I miss you
The intensity of your
Stare
The slight
Graying
Of your hair

I miss you
Your inept skill
To bring me
Crumbling
From my knees
Yet still
A single embrace
From you
Glues me back
Together
Meets all my innate
Needs

DISGUST

I miss you
Enrapture
Passion
Exhaling
Free falling
Pain
Disappointment
Mistrust
Lies
Disdain
Heart break

I miss you
So much
So very much
That if my very life
Depended on you
I would decisively
Entrust
My soul
To the lowliest minons
In
Hades

PERCEPTION

When you look at me
What do you really see?
Oh! You reminisce on
The nectar of my womanhood,
The shivering of my thighs
And
The mysteries of my flesh

But when I think of you –
I feel the lullaby of your
Heartbeat and dance to the rhythm
Of your life
As it carries my soul off into peace

When I think of you
I envision the temperature
Of your eyes
The warmth, fire, ice, cool
All reflective of your mood

When I think of you
I hear the wind of your voice,
Like the calm lapping of waves washing
Ashore
Or the turbulent swell of a violent hurricane

When I think of you
I embrace the building blocks
Of your frame
Each and every cell
That has designed you

Fashioned you
From the tips of your fingers
To the corners of your toes
The light that radiates around you
Pulses through the phone when
Your number shows

BUT, when you think of me ~
It is only,
 Always the fire of my flesh
 That you see…

REGRET

I miss you

Beyond the anger,

For it has long subsided

Even the hate has dissipated

I had glimsped you

Briefly in my mind's eye

I saw you, see me

Instantaneously

I remembered

In a sudden shocking flash

The taste of your lips

The thrust of your lips

I remembered

The smell of your hair,

Your clothes

Your cologne

Your bathed skin

And your work day musk

In a sudden instant

It all engulfed me like

A tidal wave of

Memories

Emotions

Gasps

Sighs

I do miss you

The sound

Of your thoughts

The raucous laughter

The quiet times

I miss

The nights buried deep in the

In the safety of your

Embrace

I lay snuggled and secure

Time standing so still

The world around us

No longer

Existing

Only the here

Only the now

I miss you

Your whispers

Your smile

Your walk

My heart aches

Because the absence of you

Is unbearable

And because my rhythm

Misses being synched with yours

I (_____) miss YOU!

I wish I could—

No, I tried many times to

But

Pride,

Or female willfulness

Prevents me ~

So tears escape closed eyes

As I cuddle with my

Egotism

Ego – you cold

Prickly mass is my only comfort at this time

When I wished it was you

I miss you.

Summer Nights
In Malibu
Always bring smiles
When I think of
You are the tequila
That I can't get
Enough of

Reveries
Of spending hot
Days
In salty sprays
And Cold nights
Under ominous
Lights
All shimmer like
Glints of glass in my
Rear view
Can't help but
Spread
My lips on you

Scorching touches
That burn so deep
Heels slipping from

Sweat
Grip lost
We're molten lava
Falling
Over cliffs so steep
~Licentious

Stolen time in
Darkness
Almost bring
Sunrise
Desperate moments
In passion
Meet the sun's fall
Often times,
It's the things you do
When you do
Nothing at all

It's the smell of lust
Burning
Mixed with wanton
Desire
Our yearning
Our thirst
Instinctively, it
Happens

Our bodies just fit
Oh god! What are we doing
Don't think about it
Just free fall
With it

Hands cupping curves
You caught me,
Always

No opium needed
My quest to remain
Sober in review
I've
Fallen one too many times
For the high that is you
Yet still I answer your call

The sparkle in your eyes
Shines so bright
I could see you
Know you
In the darkest place
And I could hear you
Know you
In a crowded room
And if I were blindfolded
I could feel you

My skin would know you
By your touch
Your fingers are keys

Adventure in our hands
We've got a firm hold
Air in our lungs
Whether splashing waves
Or
Unwalked paths
Arms around you,
Legs entangled
Taste in exploration
Giggles in my throat

I hate the way I feel
When I'm with you ~
Licentious

IN THE SUN

He holds my hand
Even when no one
Is looking
He takes me home
His friends I meet
His mother's sweet
The cold darkness behind me
An amazing new chapter of my life
Has just begun

We enjoy moments rare
Snapshots stay vivid
When memories fade
He's happy
To give me his love
In the sun

To travel together
Sitting close
Such an amazing feeling
To be human
Familiar
Together
And not pretend
To be
Ghost

Luminescence
Washing over my
Soul
This freedom
Has me delirious

Arm around my waist
During introductions
Proud tone in his voice
Almost presents the illusion – that-
As if
I was his one and only choice
And he's made no mistake
As if
He too can't believe this
Incredulous is the comparison
From then to this new now

His eyes they would find me
From across a crowded room
He stares at me
Only me
Sitting across from me
He talks to only me
Even when we're
Apart of a crowd

His hand reassuring me
His whispers informing me
I never have to wonder

I wasn't ready for this
Couldn't begin to imagine
This would feel
Like this
Easy to want to pinch my flesh
Try not to pretend this is real

So easy
Was it
To read the script and
Play the part
Forever real was the constant consistent
Ever recurring
Breaking of my heart

Until now…
Only my desires matter
They come second to none
You know?
I lied when I said that I preferred that way
~ No
I'd much rather this
The delicious warmth
Of this amazing love
His passionate, unrelenting love
In the sun

NOMAD

What dwelling
Shall you inhabit
If you belong not here

What nook can your
Soul seek refuge
If it knows not where

A call to come home
You shall never ever
Hear

What dwelling
Shall you inhabit
If you belong not here

Even caterpillars
Build cocoons
Free birds build nests
Cockroaches have homes
Even the homeless
Shelter pets

But
You,
You have no niche
No place where you belong
No warm safe cocoon
No quiet corner
No favorite song

No one to defend your honor
Or enforce your beliefs
No special invites
No concessions on your behalf
No compassion for your griefs

You are cursed to wander the earth
Desolate
All alone
To no one do you belong
With no place to call your own

Though many a predator
Attempted
To dim
Nay, steal your light
An innate force
Spurs
A desire in you
To persevere
To fight

Fight for the chance to see others
Happily inhabiting the métier
Carefully carved out for them
Oh, What you wouldn't give
For that simple piece of mind
But that peace of life is not for you
That pricy possession you will never
find

Content yourself
With isolation
And nurture your bones with tears

Because A call to come home
You shall never ever
Hear

For what nook can your
Soul seek refuge
If it knows not where

What dwelling
Shall you inhabit
If you belong not here…

EXTINCT

I never thought it would hurt
Like this
I never dreamed you
Would be the cause

Human this was not
More that of a beast

I never imagined
My heart being ripped from its cage
With such rage
My lungs would cease

I never thought
I could conceal tears so well

I never knew how much I appreciated the
darkness that covered my eyes
And hid my pain
My embarrassment
The rain clouds in the corners of my eyes
But I did that day

How could you dispel this venom
With my love still sitting on your lap

I never knew my voice could crack
That I would have to think back
To all the moments I saved, savored,

Sanctioned
Deflected, detoured, derailed
For you

Like creatures of the night in daylight
My mortality turned to dust

I never thought
It would be so easy for you
To dismiss
Denounce it all
All in one cold, gut-wrenching
Frivolous
Nonchalant
Wave of the hand
And
Poof!

Like an archeologist
To fossil

I never thought
That what I thought
We had
Possessed
Created
Nurtured
Could
Be eradicated
Could
Just

Die out

Wind picked the pieces
And blew them away

I never thought
We'd
Never
Exist
Almost like
Ever
Existed
Extinct

SHORT CUT PART I

Long day of learning
New ring play songs
No classroom lessons
Left that indelible an impression
Than
The Devil Round The Corner

Bus money spent on popsicle
After school
Stopping by Mrs. Davis
Was the dismissal bell rule

No 'good' bus would stop
For ones so small
How they expect us to get home?
Before dark fall and night call
Well rickety bus, it'll be you after all

Me and Tammy share middle seat
Quarter a piece we paying
Though we ain't gat that either
Popsicle stains on Yellow Elder jumpers
Shows how we prioritize our feat

Drop sleep wake up, drop sleep again
Drop in pothole wake us,
Bus getting empty
A lie we gatta bend

Bus almost reach our corner
But right before it does
It picks up couple more people,
Our lie is good as done
When Tammy screams, 'Bus Stop'
We both jump to our feet,
I scramble out first
Tammy explains to driver
"Girl in the back paying for we."

Diver looks into rear view
Girl winks at him instead
Good for us that worked out
Driver shoo's us, "Go 'head."

We never see her before
But we thankful
She like flirt
And now it was time to ramble through the
bushes
Home
"Tammy, help me tie up this skirt."

MENDACITY

He kinda just happened
Yeah
He swept in outta nowhere
His smile was beguiling
His energy was addictive
He brought heat to her cold
And
In her dry parched soil
He planted a seed
And it took hold

She wasn't looking for him
Definitely not
But lost in the darkness
He found her
He took her hand
Led her to the light
And she let him
His strength refreshing
His mind intriguing
His aura became
Her answer
His seedling anchored root

His eyes were fireflies
Where there was dusk
He brought light
Where there was monotony
He sparked excitement
Once dry barren fields
No longer existed
Now,
Green, lush fauna thrived
Leaves danced at the sound
Of his voice
She found hope in his embrace
His seedling grew a stem

She took him to corners
Of her garden
Where no feet had walked
Fences overgrown
Paths wild with brush
She wanted him to know
She pulled back her skirt
And exposed her scars
He could've critiqued,
Scoffed, ran
Instead he pruned
And patched
And watered
His seeding grew branches

Together,
They lay on soft green thick grass
His lips kissed
Her bruised tired eyes
His touch spread like ointment
Over her dry cracked emotions
His warmth
Made
The grey of her skin blush
She showed him her moon
He traced her name in stars
She let him
Read her dreams
And touch her lullaby
She saw beauty in his words
And a blanket in his arms
His seedling grew vines

She wanted him to see more
She wanted to show him
The beauty behind her pain
The cool, soothing waterfalls
Exhilarating mountain peaks
Billowing meadows
But—
He didn't want to
She didn't understand
Why wouldn't he want
To share it all with her
So, she tried again
He stifled her
She stood frozen
As his expression became
dangerous
Anger engulfed him
Dark clouds rolled in
In a flash of lightning
The beautiful rhythm of his
Voice
Now boomed like menacing
thunder
His storm blocked the sun
The Leaves trembled
A chill permeated the air
Her stars began to fall from the sky
Like the rain falling from her eyes
His vines grew thorns

His shadow became Herculean
Tender lips now grimaced
Viciously with anger
His bare teeth glistened
His breath like growls of rage
Made the earth shake
Gentle hands became fists of
Claws
And Without warning
He thrashed through her gardens
Mercilessly
Uprooting flower beds
Plowing up well laid fields

The large oak that once held their names
In love
On its trunk
He chopped
And shredded
With bare hands
She stood paralyzed
In fear and pain
Who was this monster?
What happened to his warmth?
His heart?
She couldn't move~
She couldn't save herself
So
He ran over her
His thorns slicing deep into her
She bled profusely

Somehow
She found the strength
To crawl away
And sought refuge
beneath a large branch
Of the broken oak tree
She looked up at the darkened sky
Finding herself once again
Lost in the agonizing darkness
She lay still
She was sliced from the inside out
The life seeping out of her
Returning to the earth
She gasped softly
Praying the monster
Wouldn't hear her
Find her
To finish her off
She lay still
It hurt too much to move
She could hear him screaming her
name
He was blaming *her* for the carnage
And she prayed
To die in peace
Alone
That his seedling
May die also

There's a certain calm that exists

When I'm by myself

Alone

I have time to think
Reflect

Time to lick

And

Heal my wounds

There's a certain calm that exists

    When I'm close or near to

    Where waves lap, or water trickles

    My mind undulates

    My cares float away

    My life begins to ebb and flow

    Into order

There's a certain calm that exists

    When the rain beats drums

    Against surfaces and trees

    Causing leaves to shed tears

    And soft whispers travel

    In the breeze

There's a certain calm that exists

> When no one is in my ear
>
> Telling me things I don't want to hear
>
> Pulling me here and tugging me there
>
> Putting out energy
>
> That drains me
>
> Restrains me
>
> It's oft, too much to bear

There's a certain calm that exists

> When I can fall asleep
>
> With the sun on my eyelids
>
> My dreams are in colored lights
>
> The scenes dance like fairies
>
> My mind regenerates
>
> My soul realigns
>
> I am finally at rest

There's a certain calm that exists
In the simple pleasures
That life tends to bring
Sapphire sunsets, snowflakes,
Burnt   leaves in Autumn
Eclipses   and falling stars

There's a certain
That only simple miracles in life
Can sing
And these majesties
I must endeavor
To cling
For my sanity's sake

BONUS

*SALVE

*ARSONIST

*DISGUISED

SALVE

So many years
So many tears
So many nights sitting up wondering

Pounding my brain over
The 'What Ifs'
And
The 'Why me's'

There was just
So much hate
Spent on you
So many
Photos destroyed
And
Memories burned
Or
On Hi5 deleted

I had fallen so deep
It was almost impossible
To crawl out
I had slipped down
Your precipice so steep
It was almost impossible
To see up

Then years
Brought bandages
Time spread
Antiseptic
On open blistering wounds

Absence formed a cast
Over broken bones
Clocks sewed up
The tattered fabric
In my soul
Slowly, healing
Took
Place
From the inside-
Out
Salve applied,
Bruises and scabs
Gave way for new flesh
New skin
Scars faded
And the once bitter
Memories of pain
Lost their acidic sting
The panel agreed
It was time to
Let go
And
Move on

Then
Eyes laid upon you
Words formed apologies
Clouds of rain gathered
Doubt clapped like thunder
Ghosts of the past
Flashed like lightening

In my mind I pushed you
In reality
Lips meshed

In all the
Remodeling
Resurfacing
And
Replastering
Of gray
I missed that sprig
Of green

Hard as I tried to
Sterilize my
Life of you
Tried to
Bleach your color
From me
Tried with all my might to foster the
Concrete emotions
I had gardened

Your landscape
Had planted
A rose
That now
Flourished
Through stone
With thorns so protective
It was unable to be uprooted

Like magnet to steel
I'm drawn to
You

Strong arms
Burly torso
Rugged beard
Beguiling smile

Your eyes would
Lock me
That stare
Would pull me

A course would
Guide me
Instinctively
Unconsciously
Into your path

Anticipation builds
I wonder what
Scent will
Intoxicate me
This time

Which cheek will
Be blessed to rub
Against your beard
I hold my breath
 The seconds pass more
Deliberately
The earth decelerates on its
Spin
Faces move in slow motion
In time you stick a pin

Your lips give way to beautiful teeth
As your smile
Wills the world to stop
To give us this moment
Uninterrupted
Undisturbed
Unremitting

Even if I wanted to stop
Myself
I couldn't
There's a power greater
Than mine

That compels
Me
Propels
Me

A force that
Drives me
Entices me
Into your
Embrace

And my atoms
Implode
Primary Explosion
As my skin
Touches yours
Spontaneously,
My nerves are
Set ablaze

Your accelerant of cologne pours
All over me
Coats me
You speak words
That I cannot hear
But your voice
Booms into me
Secondary Explosion

You don't understand
How in this moment
You can
Fully control me
Every emotion
Every thought

Should you take
My hand
And lead me away
To God knows where,
I would not protest
Nor challenge you
Nor make any inquiries
It matters not
I'm yours
My mortality is melting
Into a pile
At your feet
But my aura
You've snatched it
And tucked it away
In your back pocket

You turn
And kiss my cheek
I was not expecting
Your lips
On my skin
Like fanned flames
The fire rises higher

The inferno continues to devour me
Consume me
I am engulfed
And I love it
I long for it

My bones
Are now cinder
Ashes lay where I once
Stood
In a shaker you placed
My soul
And expertly combined
Ingredients
Molotov Cocktail'd me
Your lips
The lighter

Then
Without caveat
A Cold
Wind sweeps in

As your embrace loosens
And icy air passes between us
To swirl my ashen bones
And flesh
Together

And my core cries out
Like tortured souls
In the Underworlds
It rebels

I don't want you to
Let go
To ever let me
Go
Yet I know that you must

Someone is waiting on you
I too
Must leave
But every
Majestic
Winged creature
In heaven
Knows
How much
I can't wait

To be drawn
Like magnet
To you
Again
To be
Intensely frenzied
Passionately emblazoned
By you
Again
My Arsonist

DISGUISED

Delicate are the wonders
That bring me joy
Minute the baubles that
Supply me with pleasure
When fantasy tastes so much
Better than reality
The depth of contentment
Stands far too deep to measure
But no one believes this…

Fragile is the tightrope that I walk
But no one sees this…
A fine unsteady line between light and
Darkness
The darkness is deep
It's frightening
Void of buoyancy
The darkness vacuums and sucks in
Making it near impossible to emerge
The darkness is agonizing
An abyss of anger and hostility
Impatience and depression

Thus the choice is obvious
To dwell vivaciously in the light
The sound of birds
The warmth of fam and friends
Sunshine and sunsets
Sparkling blue oceans
The laughter of children
Champagne bubbles
Blue skies and even rain

You awake each day with the darkness
Yapping at your heels
Beckoning you to veer
Close enough to the edge
Just close enough for its tentacles
To snake around your ankles
And drag you into its cold dank lair

So you awake each day
Walking that tight rope a bit stronger
Willing body and mind
Each day your smile broader than before
You try to touch others positively to make

The light
Radiate brighter
You choose words of icing and sprinkles
To taste better in the ear
Rather than lie still
And allow the darkness to feast on
Your laziness,
Your weakness,
You fight for the light

When along comes the darkness
No longer an engulfing, permeating mass
It has taken shape and form
It's disguised itself in clothes
Because the harder you fight
The more deceptive it becomes
Each time the voice and form are different
But you know it...

Sometimes it's disguised
To discredit your energy
Now matter how hard you work
How early you show up

Or how late you leave
How sick you come and perform
It tells you do more, be more, you're just Not up to
Standard,
It grades and degrades you, it evaluates you
Often unfairly
It rates and berates you
It advances others over your talent and
Dedication
It amplifies the minuscule flaws
And ignores the magnificence of your
Progress
It seeks to break you
Still you walk tall on your tight
Rope never looking down

So
The darkness attacks your galaxy
It tells those around you that your words Are fake,
disingenuous; lies
Your smile is counterfeit
And that your light is artificial
Your walk is haughty
Your style is unacceptable

Your desire to not conform, confirms your Conceit
And little by little the people begin to buy Into the
darkness
Those people, they don't know how Excruciatingly
Hard it is for you to keep the Lights on
That you breathe light out
Because you need it to breathe back in
They just don't know how hard you
Searched to find *you*, to be *you*
Authentically *you*, comfortable *you*
The *you* that can complement, support,
Uplift and enrich with the purest sincerity
Those people that *you* bolstered, listened to,
Prayed for and with, cried with, even fed
Those people *you* loved
Rather than stand by *you* in the light, in the
Laughter, in the warmth
Instead gravitated obligingly to the frigid
Evil darkness

You've been in that darkness
Many times before
You know the danger
You have the stitches
Some wounds will never heal
Some are cut way too deep
You've been stifled and strangled
Many times you almost didn't make it out
You almost gave in, you almost gave up
It's so much easier to surrender to it
And let it feast on your mind
Control your thoughts and actions
Staying in the light is the fight
But the rewards are far greater
The fruit ~far sweeter

So understand that
Because of *my* light
The smile *I* wear is from a gratified place
A place of peace
A harmony God carved into the chambers
Of my existence
The tranquility I exude is the prize from the
Wars I've fought and won

My words of milk and honey were birthed
From the stinging verbal assaults lashed
(Un)Consciously at *me* for being *me*
My walk is my victory dance
A touchdown to the elements that I hurdled
Over to get here
My style is authentically me, as I envision Me
And I conform not to the cages built in clone images

So when I reached out to you
My embrace, I endeavored, would be an
Adhesive
I hoped to piece you back together,
Bandage you up and spur you on
So that you could fight a little harder
A little longer
And way stronger

I know what it must seem like, but
There is joy when you emerge from the Darkness
And I will you to want it
To See it
Give yourself a chance to
Enjoy it
Embrace it
Appreciate it
And realize the fight is worth it if you just
Don't look
Down into the
Darkness

9 798607 894672